REVOLT OF THE CRASH-TEST DUMMIES

a lynx house book
EASTERN WASHINGTON UNIVERSITY PRESS

REVOLT OF THE

CRASH-TEST DUMMIES

POEMS BY
JIM DANIELS

Cover photograph by Luke Miller, from the London Science Museum

Cover design by A. E. Grey

Library of Congress Cataloguing-in-Publication Data

Daniels, Jim, 1956–

Revolt of the crash-test dummies : poems / by Jim Daniels.

  p. cm.

"A Lynx House book"

ISBN 1-59766-024-8

I. Title.

PS3554.A5635R48 2007

811'.54—dc22   2006101236

Eastern Washington University Press

Spokane and Cheney, Washington

CONTENTS

REVOLT OF THE **CRASH-TEST DUMMIES**

1

the Ward Cleaver in me. The Pat Boone
in me. The K-Mart in me. The Slurpee
in me. The boiled hot dog, the mac
and cheese in me. The Tang in me.
You bring out the Hamburger Helper
in me. The Twinkie, the Cheese Whiz
in me. You bring out the bowling trophy
in me. The student council in me.
The parliamentary procedure in me.
The missionary position in me.
You bring out the canned vegetables,
the Jell-O in me. The training wheels in me.
You bring out the lawn edger in me.
The fast-food drive-thru window in me.
The Valu Meal in me. You bring out
the white briefs in me. The cheap beer
and weak coffee in me. You bring out
the 15% tip chart in me. The sad over-
weight weekend golfer in me.
You bring out the ex-smoker in me.
The jumper cables in the trunk with flares
and the red flag to tie to the window
in me. You bring out the Tony Orlando
in me. The canned situation-comedy
laughter in me. The elevator music
in me. The medley of TV-commercial
jingles in me. The Up with People
in me. I've come to a complete stop
at the STOP sign. I've got
my emergency flashers on.
My doors are locked, baby,
but I'm waiting for you.

11:34 p.m., and the rich are peering up,
searching for the moon. Okay, not *all*

of them. I ate Wilma for breakfast.
Tomorrow I'll eat Fred.

My neighbors' air conditioner just
kicked on, buzzing angry wasp.

Their windows stare dark and smug.
Sleep, sleep, you dirty lying bastards.

Okay, that was uncalled for.
My late great-aunt's window air conditioner

waits for me in my father's garage
300 miles away. I think of the rich

when I am too hot or too cold,
but I simply eat when I am hungry.

My stomach just galloomped—
a little guy in there wearing goggles,

spraying walls with acid. I turn up
my music a notch. Two notches.

I asked for a rooster for my eighth birthday
but got two sick songbirds who missed

the department store and died
within a week. I killed my first

fish with a hammer. Good days
I want to be that stubborn.

The moon is a gong. It's the breath mint
I choked on before going in to ask

for a raise. I almost didn't type that.
They say *I'm* making too much noise.

My fingers sizzle on the knob.
I said *pleased to meet you* five times today.

I even said *bless you* when somebody sneezed.
Did I please you? I want to ask

somebody. My neighbors? My wife?
I think *negligent* should be an article

of clothing. I played piano beautifully
in their living room in a nightmare I had.

No visible moon tonight. The gong I hear
is my heart beating. Is yours beating too?

Okay.

It isn't brain surgery.
But then again, what else is?

Two dogs are company.
Three's a lot of shit.

Isn't lingerie a great word?
I mean, it's got "linger" in it.

What came first, the nook
or the cranny?

A dead squirrel was the first
heating pad.

Ice it, or heat it? Even the doctors
get confused. That leads me

to inflamed. See, that's a great
word because it's got "med" in it.

And lamé! And inf, an obscure name
for a Danish elf.

I want to be a Danish elf in lamé
who's finally off his meds.

I picked three flowers today.
They quietly share the same vase.

Generals calculate the best weather
for killing. They listen to the voices
of satellites and the wind tunnel
of the president's skull.
> They should hire my great aunt
> Martha's arthritic joints.

The generals calculate
the appropriate amount of uppers
and downers pilots should take
for optimum performance.
> They should hire my brother Steve,
> a truck driver.

The generals calculate
the appropriate syntax and diction
with which to smokescreen and snow-job.
> They should hire my brother-in-law
> Todd, the appliance salesman.

> Martha, Steve, and Todd—my country's
> brain trust—agree on the lunch menu,
> and on keeping things in the family
> where no physical violence is allowed.

The generals eat the latest in sugary cereals.
They are anxious to wipe that smirk
off somebody's face.

The dummies drive off in clown cars,
disappear in the distance.
The generals wipe their glasses.
They cough. With each cough
a door slams shut.

I swing the back door open, and it tears a hole
in the green canvas awning sagging with snow.
Two mourning doves on the black wire briefly flutter,
then land again, never straying far. We didn't use
the feeder this winter. Last fall, we cut down
the dead crab apple tree we'd hung it in.
I walk to a meeting where I will vote
on firing somebody. She will have trouble
finding another job. I shook the snow off
the awning and onto the ground. Too late
for the awning. What's she doing this morning?
Stroking her little white dog and killing herself
with mounds of snacks, knowing what's
coming? Their nest sits in the big pine tree
across the street—the illusion of a simple life.
We've already consulted a lawyer. She has too,
if she's smart. Is she the scraggly robin
that never flew south? My children in snow pants
and boots have waddled onto the school bus.
The tree stump's buried by snow, but we know
it's there. We didn't feed the birds this winter.
We assume they survived without us,
though some surely died, like all birds
and people. Her dog, just part of the problem,
one variant of her daily late arrival. I complicate
the fresh snow with footprints. The pine tree shivers
down a dusting that melts against my face.
I'm thinking about the awning.
What will it cost to fix, eh, love birds?

They say if you just strap weights
around your ankles and wrists
and carry on
        you will be stronger.
They say if you just strap weights
to your earlobes and testicles
you will hear
        your true love call your name.
They say if you just carry a coffin
above your head every day of your life
animals will love you
        and you will accept death.
They say if you just wear a cast-iron hat
and tip it to your enemies
you will learn forgiveness
        or vengeance.
They say if you strap on a lead belt
and listen to Chubby Checker records
you will fuck
        with dignity.
They say if you fill your mouth with gold
and chew raw meat like bubblegum
you will be both seen
        and heard.
They say if you replace your hair
with steel rods and comb it
with a garden rake
        it won't blow in the wind.
They say if you bench-press a small automobile
you will be crushed.
        They say there are limits
to what weights can do.

They say the weight
of the heart minus the weight of the soul
cannot be lifted.

They say in the land of 3000 dreams
strong men and strong women
will have weak children
from being constantly lifted
from the weight of expectation
from the heavy words
raining down on them.

Perhaps they should shoot him up
with his own shit. Smash it
into a giant syringe, push the plunger.
Or inject liquid explosives and blow him
to smithereens. Maybe inject the stuff
into his eyeball or the tip of his dick.
Maybe zoom in. Splatter the camera lens
with his entrails. Maybe the needle
should be ten feet long with spikes
on the side. Maybe have a child
do the honors. Maybe
a theme song with gyrations.

Robert Cosmo wet his pants
in 3rd grade. It would have been
better for him if he could at least
have been laughing—laughing
too much, not quietly alone
in the back row.

Uncle Ted's noose was velvet.
A month's worth of garbage
stacked by the back door.
In his journal, he wrote
I walked on water.

Some of us live on, smelling
of chlorine and cleanser.
Our lightbulbs last forever
and we cough our way into laughter.

While we take our snapshots,
who will notice the lone swimmer
stroking perfectly over the falls?

So, imagine the wind over the bridge again
and how she stood, leaning over the railing

as if pulled, as if she had to plant her feet
and fight against it. The wind unimpeded

rolling through the hollow, funneled,
coming after her.

✍ ✍ ✍

Her car plastered with bumper stickers
for causes old and new. No subtle thing—

bone, wish, lust. She dismissed it
as vertigo. Together you stood,

but the hawk you had promised
never appeared. And the wind cut

and the door closed behind you
and what was it she tossed off

the bridge—a button, a coin,
a paper clip or stone?

✍ ✍ ✍

She liked using the upside-down
question mark, a remnant of failed

Spanish. If everything was upside
down, she might have handled it

better. It. The failed affairs.
The illness and medication.

How would you have handled
it? Imagine her calmly connecting

the hose to the exhaust pipe,
selecting her final music.

Like she calmly laid out
birth control options

before your brief united
disappearance. It. Exhaust.

Exhaustion. Insatiable.
Her music turned loud and frenzied

to the point of static.
Then, she was ready to dance.

Sweat was sweet. Salt and sugar,
white destruction. Erosion

of the cliffs. So, that day on the bridge,
you should have suspected

the way she stood still, braced herself.
How the hawk was unwilling.

to remain silent and talk endlessly is equal
to the ability of the leaf to disintegrate
out of brilliance. The ability of the corpse
to float through clouds of grief unscathed
is only rumored. The ability of the corpse
to explain its sorry lessons in multiple languages
while juggling chain saws is unmatched
or unheard of. Always bet on the corpse,
reliable as sin, incorruptible as lies, tidy
as an oil spill, stoned as all get-out.
The ability of the corpse to weather
the storm is scrawled in blood invisible.
The ability of the corpse to disappear
is unmatched, impossible.

in the State of Grace. Not like the slack
halo worn by Albie Pearson who played center field
for the L.A. Angels then California Angels
then Anaheim Angels and they're still not sure
whose damned angels they are. Not like the tilted
halo worn by Simon Templar as "The Saint" on TV
the role that prepped Roger Moore to be James Bond.
Not like the wobbly pipe cleaner around
the distracted child in the endless Nativity play.
Not like the perfect golden arc around St. John
the Baptist's head on the plate delivered
to King Herod like a Thanksgiving turkey
in an otherwise unremarkable painting
in a dark church in Rome where my wife
tells me she's getting the creeps from the seven
deadly sins painted on the ceiling in graphic detail.
Not like the President who had the Defense Department
work with the FBI and CIA to design a lightweight
FDA-approved aerodynamic spy-proof rust-proof
halo. No, the State of Grace is seceding from the Union,
mythic and proud, slender and glowing, the haloes
are tightened another notch, leaving no room
for air, for give, for spin or sin. Turning every *mean*
into an *amen*. In the State of Grace, everyone
is governor. No one ever drops a Frisbee.
In my basement, I'm hammering away
on a thin wire, hoping they'll take me in.

2

In 7th grade, Carol Martin gave me a ring
that I used to hold a scarf around my neck
which passed as a tie back in 1969
when ties were required.

Four years before she disappeared
pregnant and Catholic still. Seven years
before her brother Matthew evaporated
one night downtown, bullet in his neck.

The ring didn't fit my finger. She wanted
to meet behind the boarded-up Dairy Queen
to kiss. To play buttons. I wanted to play button
and work my way up to plural.

I had to do my paper route, then homework,
then basketball. I had to polish my egg
of fear. I had to dance in circles in my room
like a mad dog with a happy itch.

Anything that looked like a lesson, like the thin
red-edged pages of our prayer books,
was counterfeit, or worse, Canadian. No one
would cash or save the queen or Jesus.

/ / /

Matthew died looking for a prostitute
in downtown Detroit. Carol's father held
the collection basket under my nose in church
till I smelled guilt. Sister Rosalia dropped
her habit, but wore a ring so men would know.

Know what, that she's ugly? Some-
body said. Might've been me.
I rounded aluminum foil into coins,
slipped them in my envelope, dropped
them in the basket.

God didn't approve of condoms.
The rhythm method was approved.
No one in our neighborhood had rhythm.
Rhythm or blues. Sometimes one
of the identical houses on our block

would spontaneously combust
with the fumes of bottled-up sin.
We sang "Kumbaya" in church,
holding up the hymnals
with our erect penises. Well,
some of us.

///

I rang the bells in church
at designated moments.

Jerk the wrist quickly
and whisper masturbatory prayers,

cassock and surplice dotted
with hardened wax.

I had a friend named Phallic
who had a twin brother named Chaste.

Or was it Phillip and Jake?
Or was the moon a giant communion host

and the priest a little too anxious
about the altar wine and your pretty face?

I had a dog named Wince
and two birds who killed each other

fighting over the Holy Spirit
or the Bird of Happiness.

/ / /

I should have met Carol. She had no
patience. Maybe that's obvious,
given a child named David
baptized without ceremony.

Or too much faith. Or ignorance.
Or pure uncut defiance and lust.
Half the prayers were called
"The Act of . . . Something."

I get them confused from this distance.
7 light years and 21 dark. I once took flight
in a confessional booth. I twice had sex
in a phone booth. I denied everything

three times. The cock crowed
at the drop of a school jumper.
I once believed in the Virgin birth
and pulling out early.

Matthew was in altar boys with me,
two years younger. I showed him
the ropes, the bells, the whistles.
There were no whistles. Kum-

baya, my Lord. We all wanted sex,
I assume. I heard Edith Minski joined
the nuns with her wan, defeated shuffle.
It's not true that we had no attractive nuns.

It is true they all *quit* being nuns,
disappearing off the school's map
quietly and with great murmuring
fanfare. Worth giving up God

for? It must be good. Worth dying for?
Must be bad. Who's that skinny guy,
sucked on the exhaust pipe
just because his girlfriend dumped him?

She forever became the Patron Saint of Suicide
in our liturgy, the one with slick pages,
illustrations by the monks of the order
of magazines beginning with P.

＊＊＊

Sure, I admit to residual bitterness,
a host stuck in my craw. I start out
with this neat little thing about a ring
a girl gave me once, and I end up in hell

yet again, or at least purgatory. At least
limbo. I picked dried wax off my surplice.
I wiped myself off from wet dreams.
I snuffed out candles with the giant snuffer

and turned water into wine in my father's
whiskey bottles. A dope-smoking priest
named Mike corrupted Lisa Grabel,
but that's another story. Or another chapter.

Another footnote. Another little ditty
for the folk-rock mass on Saturday night
before we retrieved our stashed bottles
and began warming the darkness.

He had lame-ass dope, but it must've been
hard for a priest to get good dope, every-
body pushing oregano and faith on you.
I think we should all make foil coins

into erotic shapes, but maybe it's just me.
There was a typo in my prayer book, or maybe
it was just—hey, Wince, come here, boy—the pages
I hollowed out to hide my dope in.

Hey, at least I never jacked off
in a confessional booth like . . .

⫻

Matthew, I rubbed your buzzed head for luck
or to cause you pain because you were younger.
How many times did I tell you how to hold the book
for the priest, how to ring the bells? To mumble

the words to the Confiteor:
Ideo precor beatum Mariam semper virginem . . .
omnes Santos, et vos fratres, orare pro me ad Dominum
bo business like show business dominoes and bee cum.

⫻

A bullet hole the size of a ring? Perhaps
I figured things out without a map,
with geographical instinct and dumb luck.
Matthew sleeping forever in the cheap Ford

he bought from Larry Carson. Shoulda
known better. For Christ's sake. Stupidity
can be outgrown. Take it from Exhibit A.
The unsolved murders of Detroit. As God

is my witness. The Our Father written
on the head of a pin. On the head
of a bullet, on the inside of a ring
some young boy threw away or gave back

or hid somewhere and couldn't find.
The organ's starting up again
for the Processional. Light the candles.
Grab the cruets and the book. Slick back

your hair and don your beatific face,
your beautific face. Your sister
a mother at fifteen and no father
speaking up.

My mother opened little windows
on her calendar and occasionally found
babies. I knew my parents never had sex
with as much certainty as . . . with as much

faith as . . . foil coins and unrepentant
smart-assism. Nobody deserved
to be born or to die. Carol had a smile
that melted my little heart into soggy

communion hosts. It wasn't me, but it coulda been.
Woulda been. Not shoulda. I didn't even
have faith in math or our kindly neighbors
from Canada with their odd coins.

If only they'd let us chew the hosts!

⁄⁄ ⁄⁄ ⁄⁄

I keep driving toward that car, but every time
I see the slumped-over body, I lock my doors
and turn around. I mumble a joke
I don't know the punch line to.

What kind of door do you suppose purgatory has?
Does it have a window in it? When somebody knocks
what are you supposed to do? Not open it waving
your money, it turns out.

Matthew had a twin brother Thomas
who had his doubts about the murder.
He had an older brother Donald. A love-child nephew
named Dave, and a dog named—

Father Mike, gimme a hit of that lame shit,
will ya? Sister Rosalia, how about a little
French kiss for old time's sake? So
there won't be any doubt about that habit,

that nasty habit. I pulled down the pants
of Saint Grief and gave it to her from behind.
Incensed with incense,
I lit her candle and I blew it out.

⁄⁄ ⁄⁄ ⁄⁄

If I keep driving toward that car, eventually
I'll skid on the ice and glide right into it.
*Eat his body, drink his blood, and we'll sing
a song of love.*

But Matthew ain't gonna sit up and say
what the fuck? or *it's only you.*
I press my thumb over the wound
and I believe what I believe.

My father mixed cement in a wheelbarrow,
lifting the shovel, turning dust into water
till it glistened. His favorite trick.
Four boys stood at a respectable distance,
punching, pushing each other into dirt.
My father was building a driveway
one square at a time. Someday, a garage.
Hypnotized by the scrape and swirl,
he'd mixed too much. We each took
an empty shoebox and set it before him.
He filled them with cement. We could
write whatever we wanted. We carved
our initials solemnly with popsicle sticks.
When the cement dried, we peeled away
wet cardboard and laid our bricks side
by side next to the house. My father
with a beer and a cigarette.
Four boys at a respectable distance.

CRY ROOM, ST. MARK'S CHURCH

In the back behind smudged glass we sat
with three other mothers and their kids.
No one was in fact crying. Or reciting
prayers. We could have been looking in

the window at the A&P or K-Mart. I was old
enough not to consider crying an option.
My little sister crawled behind the kneeler
and fell asleep. I crouched awkward in the pew.

To be caught in the cry room—I wouldn't hear
the end of it. Everyone stared down the usher
when he came in to shake his collection basket.

1963. I'd made my first communion
and begun saving my best lies
for the confessional booth. A room for sins.
A room to cry in. I watched my mother's head

loll back, snap forward. Why were we there?
Was someone going to bring us yet another
baby to take home? One woman entered late
and sat in the last of the four pews, wedging

herself into the corner to sob uncontrollably.
Other mothers stared out the stale window
at the muffled static of the mass.
Mine sighed and yanked us up and out

of there. We walked home in a fluster of spring wind.
I was hungry for a doughnut or two. Glazed,
sticky in the flimsy cardboard box with the see-through
plastic window. Did we stay long enough for it to count?
I asked. My mother carried my sister in one arm

and puffed on a cigarette with the fervor
of the newly converted. We passed the Powder
Puff hair salon and the boarded-up Dairy Queen
and the ill-fated slot-car track and the ditch

they found Larry Jarman in. I didn't cry then
and I'm not crying now. God—you had to love
the dude. God, not Larry. It might've been Larry's
mother crying in the back. Or Mary Magdalene's

distant niece. Or the victim of another immaculate
conception. All I know is that I bugged my mother
into a frenzy till she bought the doughnuts
at Oaza bakery near the drive-thru car wash

and threw the box at me and told me to shut up.
My older brothers had lied about going to early
mass. I don't know where they went, but they wouldn't
take me with them. My mother believed in miracles

and my sleeping father believed in the almighty dollar
and the nearly almighty cents. I ate two doughnuts
before we got home. The sweet glaze stuck to my lips
and face. I confess to a smile and a taunting shimmy

on the sidewalk as my brothers raced out the door
to snatch the box. My mother dropped my sister
onto the stoop, then fell to the dead brown grass
and smiled her own wistful boogaloo. You had to love him

or hate him or pretend or believe he didn't exist. The cry
room stank with soiled diapers and sweat. The hymnals
had pages ripped out, drooled and doodled on. The truth
was elusive. Why would He want criers in a separate room?

What about a room for laughers? No one laughed
in church. Even when the priest—any priest—tried out
a joke. Are there any good jokes that don't have a cruelty
to them? Cigarettes weren't as good as I'd imagined.

We haunted ourselves in the reflection of the cry-room glass.
My tiny grandmother in her tiny room watched *Mass*
for Shut-ins on her tiny TV. She might have been crying,
depending on the pain. She was my second death after Larry.

Nobody explained about Larry till I was *old enough*
to understand. The church stretched yellow police tape
around our lives like in those fancy stores where you couldn't
touch a thing. Usually, some kid started bawling, but not that day.

Oh, the sweetness of the glaze,
and how the greed made my mother smile.

I turned my tricycle upside down on the sidewalk and ran handfuls of dirt, pebbles, and twigs down the fender while spinning the pedals. I was making ice cream. I called out to the street like a happy vendor in a sitcom: *Ice cream! Get yer ice cream!* I did not have cones or cups or spoons. I had losing racetrack tickets as my legal tender. Handfuls of dirt flew out the bottom of the fender. I spun the pedals till my arm ached, my fingernails wedged with grit. No one on the long patterned street listened. Grass, cement. Grass, cement. The men were all on strike, walking picket lines or hiding out in damp, cool basements. Every house had one fan, and that fan was running uselessly. I mean endlessly. I tasted black sweat in my mouth. Three miles away, my father carried his sign. My mother had locked herself in the bathroom. Perhaps praying. Perhaps not. No one knew how long it would last. No ice cream in anybody's freezer. The wheel squeaked as I turned—the only sound in the world.

When we rang Selinsky's doorbell
        she always answered.
In her washed-out housecoat
        and flowered slippers,
she scanned the street,
        a lighthouse with no ships at sea.
Her husband Ed smoked cigars.
        He'd been dead for years
but his empty butt pot clanged
        on the porch when we jumped
to hide behind her bushes.

        Radio contest! You're a winner!
we shrieked into her phone.
        She sat on her porch, waiting
for the envelope that never arrived.
        No one was calling *us*
to step outside our lives.
        The magnetic pull of cruelty
left us kissing bitter metal, hissing
        delight like cruel scientists

while we ourselves dug into cereal boxes
        for FREE GIFTS
shoveled snow for quarters
        and shoplifted at the variety store.
We told dirty jokes and dared each other
        not to laugh.
We didn't ask what our fathers did.
        We knew which way the smokestacks blew,
patiently waiting to draw us in.
        If we were coins
you could have called every flip.

We ditched each other,
            practicing abandonment.
We played Kill the Guy with the Ball.
            We took it. Our knees bled
from botched prayers. We slid across
            cracked cement into every base
called home.

At the doors of our houses
            we did not knock or ring bells.
We sang the high mass
            of each other's names.
We practiced the art of No Mercy
            and the sport of The Grudge.
We slit our favorite teacher's tires.

Alex, the manager, turned off the pale neon,
locked the sliding glass windows,
and cranked up Hendrix on the stereo

in the back room of the Dairy Queen
owned by his father. He wailed on
air guitar while I wielded a mop

against the sticky floors and gathered up
the cold wet rags of the day, while I mixed
sugar and water for tomorrow's slushes—

that, and food coloring, is all they are.
People shelling out good money
to get those killer headaches, go figure.

"With the power of soul anything is possible."
I was fifteen and just beginning to figure.
Alex sprouted gold chains across chest hair

while I shaved fuzz off my upper lip and stared
through Renee and Crystal's white uniforms.
Alex wanted to be in a band of gypsies,

but all signs pointed to a lifetime of slushes,
double dips, Mr. Misty's, Fudge Brownie Delites,
chocolate-covered bananas and Dilly Bars.

"We Gotta Live Together." He forced me
to clap along, though I lost the rhythm
in feedback and static. Hendrix would be dead

soon enough, no surprise to anyone. Alex chained
by gold, even if it was a little sticky.
I made 85 cents an hour, and my loyalty

was often questioned. "We Gotta Live
Together." I jumped on trash in the dumpster
to make room for more. He rubber-banded cash

with his pudgy fingers. I was grateful
to be there, on top of the trash. Hendrix's
guitar screeching out the open back door.

one day at lunch. He should have
been getting stoned in the gravel parking lot
or dry-humping some girl against
the bricks behind Auto Shop.

Charles Holmes blew up the chem lab,
cracking one of those huge black tables
in half. His glasses shattered, cut
his eyes. His hair singed off. He could
not hear well for some period of time.

Charles Holmes blew up the chem lab.
We heard the boom in the parking lot
and laughed. The chem teacher was locked
in his office with one of our classmates.
Coitus interruptus chemistrus.

Charles Holmes blew up the chem lab
against all expectation, even his. We
looked up at the sound, then returned
to whatever small sins we were committing,
most of which involved inhaling deeply.

Charles Holmes blew up the chem lab
and somebody lost his job and some-
body left school and never returned
and somebody named Charles Holmes
returned in two weeks without benefit

of eyebrows. Me, I was failing chemistry
and benefited from the diversion.
The substitute relied entirely on the textbook.
Cheating was rampant and effective.

Charles Holmes blew up the chem lab.
We nodded then when he passed
in the hall. Skinny pimply-faced ass-
kissing geek that he was. She hadn't
been the first one to eat lunch

in that office, it turned out. She'd refused
to go out with any of us. Charles
Holmes got a date to the prom and lived
happily ever after, as far as we know.

Nobody believes my high school
offered a class called OUTDOOR CHEF.
The yearbook carried a picture of us firing up
the barbecue in the parking lot. This was before
the Invention of the Gas Grill. Before they
raised the drinking age back to 21. Jimi Hendrix
burned his guitar at Monterey then died shortly after,
bumming us out in OUTDOOR CHEF. It was only
a one-semester course so we had to cram. Charcoal lighter
was routinely abused. We spelled our names
on the sidewalk and lit them, like pissing
in snow. Our teacher was Mrs. Reynolds. Enormous
and cheerful and in retrospect willfully ignorant and alcoholic.
It was a difficult class to teach—no textbook. Mr. Farwell,
our principal, needed higher graduation rates, courses
to shunt problem kids into. Not one fight in OUTDOOR CHEF,
despite having the toughest guys in the school bunched together
around the grills. Class was often outside, even in winter.
Class was often cut, long wild hair disappearing into snow
toward the parking lot. Joints often snaked between us,
smoke blending with burning meat. I learned a lot
about cooking chicken and pork. See, those are
important things. You can get sick not cooking
them long enough, and make others sick too.
Neighbors would never come over for a cookout again.
My apron had some crude joke about a hot dog on it.
So did everyone else's. I can't begin to express how clever
we were. We cooked a whole turkey for Thanksgiving
and served it to Mr. Farwell and Mr. Stark,
the assistant principal/hit man. He said he could've used
a course like that when he was in school. They did not get sick.
It was a festive occasion until we let a live turkey

loose in the main hallway. No girls in OUTDOOR CHEF,
though you might have guessed that. The jocks
were subdued and serious about remaining eligible.
Our school had few jocks to spare. The rest of us
were lighting each other's long hair on fire
and thinking that was a fine joke.
Okay, Eddie Bucco did get stabbed with a skewer
but we all agreed it was an accident. We enjoyed waving
our hands above the hot coals—none of us bothered
with winter gloves. The last day of class, Jackie Smoker
brought in his cheap electric guitar and tried to imitate
Hendrix blasting from his nearby car radio.
He messed up his hands bad, but for awhile it was
beautiful. Even now, I am full of self-mockery
and loathing. The truth was that for many of us
having our own barbecue would indicate
a successful life. Mrs. Reynolds had gone to college
to teach Home Ec. We should have treated her better. Her
and everybody else. Yes, it's on my transcript with a C—
our final had some math on it. The wind blew ash and smoke
into the air just like at the factory down the road.
We had to provide our own briquettes. There's an enormous
number of things you can cook outdoors. The only class
in which we believed what the teacher told us.
Because we could see. That, and gym.
We chewed gum outside and threw it against
the school building. Mr. Farwell gave most of us
diplomas. I don't know how many years
OUTDOOR CHEF was offered.
You could not burn your marshmallow
on the test. That, when all we wanted
was to go up in flames.

I lived in an ancient motel turned into efficiencies
barely big enough for the double bed.
Two electric burners and a sink.
Four friends from Michigan came to visit.
So happy to see them, I poured beer
over their heads, up their sleeves. They in turn
did not hurt me. I'd started smoking again.
I blamed the whole state of Ohio. In that small town
you could walk everywhere and nowhere
and in between. Three bars—two with the word
"Dead" in their names. The wind smacked us upside
our drunken little heads. One friend, a woman,
shared the bed with Marc. The rest of us lay
on indoor-outdoor carpet in a U-shape around them.
We listened to each other breathe in that stinky room.
Months later, in the middle of a shower, the entire wall
of plastic tiles crashed down on me. It could happen
that quickly. An awkward bruise, an unfamiliar
number, a misplaced ring. When the phone rang, I didn't
answer it. Nobody did. They might've done something
under the covers, Marc and Lee Ann. The sound
would've been a blessing. Maybe I heard it, maybe I didn't.
In the morning, I made eggs and instant coffee
and Tang. We stood without coats in the ravaged parking lot.
I lived in #2. There was no #1. We smoked and coughed
and laughed till they drove back to Michigan
and I walked down to work at the Korner Grill.
Maybe they'd stolen Marc's K and stuck him
with the C. At least they didn't add an E on Grill.
My ex was back in Michigan—her name ended in E.
The woman I'd followed to Ohio was lost in between
the O and o where the clouds had numbers

and the hills were either imaginary
or man-made or laced with unknown
chemicals. I slept at the foot of the bed
and was almost never happier. Four friends.
If I was a dog, I'd have licked their feet.
The U can be a beautiful letter, softly catching
falling things. The room key, attached
to a large plastic motel, jabbed my pocket
like a worn knife. My friends convinced me to use
my porch light for its radiant yellow,
its optimistic glow. In case somebody might
come home, even if it was only me.

In Amsterdam my friend Dr. Zero
put the Dutch equivalent of a quarter
into a machine to watch some fat hairy
zombie fuck a pig. A real pig. The screen
was tiny, but not tiny enough, for he invited me
to take a peek, and, given my only chance to watch
a man fuck a pig, I took it. I liked Holland
because we could also call it The Netherlands
and call the people Dutch so we had a lot of options
while smoking legal marijuana in a club
that warned us not to shoot up in the bathroom.
Everybody draws the line somewhere. Perhaps
you drew it a few lines back, and I'm whispering
my sins to a dusty screen and I won't be getting
any penance for my trouble. Dr. Zero was sufficiently
disgusted and chose not to watch the one
with the donkey. Not that I hadn't put a few guilders in—
that's it, *guilders*! What a great name for money.
And they have the best dimes in the world.
Smaller than ours. It's great to come upon one
in the deep lining of a coat, walking home
from the hash bar knowing you're *not* broke—
yes, I'd used up all my change at the arcade
watching variations on a theme. Twenty-five years ago.
We didn't get tattoos like we'd threatened to,
and it's a good thing, seeing as how trendy they are
now. The past is like a bad back—not subtle enough
to haunt anyone. Ten years ago a doctor told The Doctor
he might have AIDS and Dr. Zero obsessed
about that prostitute in Amsterdam he spent five
minutes with, even though she'd unrolled
a condom on him. It turned out he had

chronic fatigue syndrome. Every story
is a long story. We didn't shoot up. We didn't
fuck any animals. We told each other the truth
most of the time. I haven't seen him
in sixteen years. The world is a bad joke.
Sometimes we laugh because we think
we're supposed to. When I showed him
the Dutch dime, he took it and swallowed it
so I'd really be broke. I forgave him.
I made a wish.

My father dances to "Spanish Eyes"
with my brother's new bride. He holds
her hand as tight as he held
his retirement papers. My mother's spine

twists in a light blue dress. She loved
my brother's first wife. She eyes my father's
smooth steps, the paper tablecloth
shredding beneath her.

The groom's not snorting coke in the john
this time. He's sipping ginger ale.
The bored dj's eating meatballs, dribbling sauce.
My mother's foot bounces. My father squeezes

a smile for the camera while the bride stares
stiffly into the ruffles of his shirt.
Some cynic taps his spoon against a glass
till my brother cuts in for a sloppy kiss.

My father slumps gladly away.
My mother applauds against her drink.
The DJ ups the tempo. My father glances
at his watch. My mother covers his wrist

with her bony fingers. The bride and groom
stuck alone on the dance floor. We are happy
for them. But not enough to do The Hustle.

My father uses the pill sorter
he used to fill for his own father.
Day by day, morning and night,
multicolored dice lifted from the slots.

He downs them from a shot glass
I stole from a bar
that spelled Club with a K
the week before my grandfather died.

You could make tiny ice cubes
with it, or store small speckled eggs.
It'll last forever, so it's mine
next. I'm already taking a couple

every day. Our imaginations
never included bitter aftertaste
and imagined grievances. The three
of us built a fire together once.

We glided over ice, scarves flying.
We stored our smudged truths
in the cellar. We waved away
all assistance. My father squints

at the label on his new pill bottle.
It says he'll be dizzy
for awhile, but he'll get used
to it. *When I die*, he says.

Together in the kitchen, we shake
our heads. His tilts, and swallows.

Some of the jobs these machines replaced were difficult, boring, or
dangerous; others were good jobs that paid well and workers enjoyed.
     —Robotics exhibit, Henry Ford Museum, Dearborn, Michigan

My father, my children, my wife, and I
were recruited to work on a toy car assembly line.
My son placed the yellow plastic frame onto
the conveyor. My wife snapped the red body onto
the frame. My father snapped the blue seats in.
I pushed the front end on. My daughter cranked
the conveyor, controlling the speed. We each had
a small box of parts. The museum employee
in her perky red vest started a Chaplinesque sound track,
and we began, working smoothly till she instructed my daughter
to crank faster, and we got backed up, tossing half-
formed cars to the side. *Faster*, she kept telling her.
We ran out of parts just as the music stopped. The employee counted
the good cars and the bad. Bad outnumbered good. My son
asked if we could keep the cars. She said, *No*—in fact, we had
to take them apart, so that others could put them together again.
My father and I had worked on assembly lines
where if you couldn't keep up, you were fired.
Where time controllers assessed how long each job
should take and set the line speed. The family
that took our places asked me to videotape the whole thing.
I wish I could say I was making this up. Inside, I felt
the old humiliation throbbing again in my stooped back.
I hated this woman, bossing my daughter around.
I told her I wanted to see my union rep, trying
to keep it light. But she had a script to stick to
and was probably making minimum wage herself.
She didn't explain to us what we were supposed
to take away from our experience. Just not the cars.

Wonder Bread builds strong bodies twelve ways

We toured the Wonder Bread factory,
our blue and yellow Scout uniforms jittering down
the drab aisles of hum and clang.

At the end of the line, we were allowed
our taste of Detroit's assembly-line communion.
The workers silent as we passed, staring over

our heads, numb with what they could not share.
In their own uniforms, bare of arrows
and awards, they disappeared into white bread.

Back on the bus, I was drunk with the smell
of warm bread emerging from giant ovens.
In the stores, the spongy white loaves

were covered in balloon-patterned plastic. What were
the twelve ways? Eyes closed, my friend stroked
his cheek with a warm slice. Wouldn't it be great

to work here? he said. When we toured the Stroh's
Brewery years later, he said the same thing.
They offered no tours of auto plants,

yet that was where we ended up, parking
our first cars in the enormous lined lots,
fenced in, protected. Wouldn't it be great

if communion tasted like this?
Tony said. At home, my mother baked bread
on rare occasions, her misshapen yeasty loaves

waiting warm in the kitchen after school.
But they hardened quickly, the odd shapes
sloppy for sandwiches—she made at least a dozen

every night for school and work lunches, an assembly line
of peanut butter and jelly, bologna and mustard,
brown paper bags initialed for morning send-offs.

That bakery is now the Motor City Casino,
slots and chips clattering away the ghosts
of loaves. The brewery's gone too, by the way,

by the way, by the way, way side.
A money factory, what could be purer
and sicker? I'm driving my car past

that grand old factory, a building saved
by greed, a rare Detroit victory against rubble.
Twelve ways. I hold up my three fingers

to recite the old scout oath. I make the sign
of the cross and recite the two prayers
I remember. What I remember is

you weren't supposed to chew.
Just swallow and take it on faith.

4

All our friends were still alive
and half our grandparents and 3/4
of our old teachers and 96%
of our enemies. Life had a full head

of clean, dark hair waving ostentatiously
in the wind, the tangled greeting
of our youthful flags, survivors
only of minor skirmishing

and improper folds. Our report cards
were full of deliberate incompletes
and perfect attendance. *Here*, we waved,
when our names were called, *we're here*.

/ / /

In 1989 we were AWOL from our old lives
and newly married and hiding in a small town
in Umbria, Italy, like diamonds on the long
perfect necks of the beautiful young.

Out the large, arched window of our ancient house,
the world spread itself humbly at our feet.
April, the hillside's plush green eruptions liquid

with curves and sex, the sparkling silver sweat
of olive leaves, the stoic stone town in the distance,
layered circles of walls to mark centuries of illusions
while we gloated over our warm, moist skins.

/ / /

The bowl of blood oranges, and lemons big as grapefruits,
bigger! and the flowers blooming in long clay planters,
and the flealess cat who daintily gnawed our cheese rinds,
and the neighbor who never closed her door despite the cold,
and the delirious stink of wood smoke on our clothes,

and the friendly scorpions who lifted their stingers
in joyful acknowledgment of our beauty. Okay,
I'm laying it on thick—it was the only way we could
lay it on then. Ecstatic over one black truffle
and obscure cheeses layered in mold and thick red wine
in refillable jugs. Lemons big as the sun, and sweet!

/ / /

Exclamation points rattle loose and brittle in a box.
73% of our friends still alive, and $\frac{1}{2}$ our parents
and $\frac{1}{4}$ of all our old teachers and 96% of our enemies.

No one from that village sends us Christmas cards
anymore. Our children's voices echo sweet
and shrill off the cracked cement of this American city
where we love them 100%, exactly. The lemons

were enormous. Mysterious green shadows
drew us in for four months of 1989. How many
opportunities like that do you get in one life?

One life? One life? We'll never go back. Let the photos
fade, as they must. Though if we wandered down
again to Palmela's house, would she answer the door,
thirty-five now, her parents retired or dead,

and let us use the pay phone in her garage,
the only line out from that small village then?
Would she remember running up the hill,
pony tails flying, to tell us breathlessly

that we had a phone call from America,
and how we cried afterward, numbly hanging
up, speechless with grief so easily translated,
her mother leading us gently out the door
and into another country.

The conservatory gave out packets
of mystery seeds to the kids
for finishing Plant Bingo
one Sunday morning. We couldn't find
the vanilla bean but filled it in anyway.

My mother spaces out her pain pills
to keep from getting hooked.
She keeps a chart and brags
about the long gaps. When I took acid,
I bragged about my "greatest hits."

We planted the seeds in our yard
and miniature flowers bloomed,
so tiny and delicate we couldn't even
see them from the back window.

My mother is an expert in pain. *On a scale*
of one to ten, how would you rate it?
She's into fractions. She downs her
pills from shot glasses lining the counter,
spaced out. I took mystery pills
just to see where they took me.
Flowers for elves, I called them.

The children bend down, their easy crouch
mocking my stiff knees. Praying
is the other thing my mother does.
She plans imaginary trips with my father
for when she *gets better*. Those seeds
could have grown giant bean stalks
or poison ivy or poppies.

I once sang a love song in Spanish
in a crowded bar to an unsuspecting
teenaged hooker. I have become weatherman
and seer to my children. I never stole a pill
from my mother. She kneels over the side
of her bed with a rosary, following her spine's
harsh curve.

Anything could be true, even afterward,
talking about the trip with fellow travelers.
Let's get small y'all. Every car I've owned
has returned to zero. I suppose that's bragging.
I inhale the tiny flowers with my miniature nose.
My children's enormous faces crowd around
as I squeak, *Don't try this yourself.*

(*Hope*)

I hung blue curtains, framing
January rain. A room for *her*.
If she were to be born, if she lived,
if she fooled the harmonica-blowing grim reaper
doing his fandango out in the puddles,
I wanted to give my daughter
that name. I climbed down from the ladder
to feel her stir inside you.

Across the street, a hand dropped
a small vial into an open car window. I cursed
the view. Should we move—where?
I called the police again.

The next day in the hospital's safe glare,
we named her Rosalie, not caring what it meant.
I had wanted to shout into cold rain streaming down,
threatening snow, without getting shot.

Our daughter turns one today. Soon our lights
will click on automatically, darkness
voracious. You nurse her to sleep.
The exotic word for hope rises
unspoken. We are still here.

Today my son realized someone's smarter
than him. Not me or his mom—
he still thinks we know everything.
One of the other kids, Nathan, made fun
of him at the computer for screwing up
at the math game. Other kids laughed.
2nd grade. *I'm never gonna be as smart*
as him, he says.

                         I'm never gonna be smart
as half my students if we're talking IQs.
He doesn't want me to explain.
He wants me to acknowledge
that he's dumb. He's lying in bed
and taking his glasses off and on,
trying to get them perfectly clean
for the morning. I'm looking around
his dark room for a joke or some
decent words to lay on him. His eyes
glassy with almost-tears.
The world wants to call on him.
I take his hand in mine.

My daughter Rosalie cradles my head
in her tiny lap like I'm a fluffy something.
Yesterday we watched a man beat his dog.

I stood speechless on the crumbling sidewalk
holding my children's hands. Today, she wouldn't
put her game away. She cried for an hour instead.

You can't walk on the sky, my son Ramsey says.
The guy hitting his dog stalks them both.
We gave our dog away

when we had two children under two
and he started crapping on the rugs.
My daughter's soft spot is just about closed up.

She put the game away once she caught her breath.
Why is it so important to put a game away?
One stupid question, and the whole world

crumbles. Sometimes a man kicks a dog
and you get a black smudge nobody can erase.
He glared at us as we passed till we all

looked away. My little girl's holding my head
in her lap. My son is thinking about the sky.
He uses the white crayon to try to cover

his mistakes. We pretend it erases them.
I'd like to imagine we can ignore some things.

I'd like to take that white crayon and draw a line
up to the sky, where it could fade like all things,
remain like all things.

What's an esophagus? My son fingers
broken toys and watches loud TV.
He's in for overnight testing. They'll stick
a tiny camera on a tube up his nose,
down his throat. *Ask the doctor.*

Next to us, a man in a Red Wings jersey
tight over his round belly leans back
and yawns while his son blankly flips
through a book. They've driven in from Detroit.
Back to check on his new ticker, the man smiles.
The kid's had a transplant.

No windows here. Rain predicted. Elevators
color-coded. The tube slides in smoothly.
My son, under for the first time, the thick dirt
of fake sleep. The Red Wings are off
to a good start. My son knows what
a heart is. They should have won the Cup
last year. Cameras can go anywhere now.

The man in his red and white jersey
skates down the ice into sleep.
Our sons curl around their young lives.
It's easy to get lost in here. My son vomits
the cherry popsicle after he wakes.

The man does not have to tell me
we are lucky, but he wishes us *more* luck.
The orange plastic chairs are bolted
in place, but we are leaving now.

In dank Italian churches, we loaded machines
with lira to light candle-smoked saints.

In front of Caravaggio's *The Calling of St. Matthew*
I emptied my pockets.

/ / /

I am taking the crib down. It won't be used
again—not by us. My children are three and two.

This morning I woke to the light of their voices
talking in bed about the short lives of flowers.

I am weeping onto my power screwdriver.
I wipe their tiny smudges from the rails.

/ / /

In a bar in Bowling Green, Ohio,
I denied my name to a rugby player

until she doubted her drunken memory
that I had slept with her the year before.

Nothing is clear as Caravaggio's light.
One small gesture, and it's all a blur.

We'd stood at the door, closing time, checking
out the passing bodies till we were alone.

What would she have said if I'd acknowledged
that night in my cramped efficiency, too drunk

to pretend we enjoyed the clash? In the morning,
plastic shower tiles crashed down on me.

/ / /

No one has ever called *me* like that.
In Italy that winter, my wife and I looked out

one big window for the tiny mailman. We rubbed
the Buddha's belly and bought cut flowers in the market.

We looked for signs to save us. After our money
ran out, we just stared into murky shadow.

In a hilltop cemetery, we visited the faces of the dead
shaded by lush trees, high walls, wind hush.

/ / /

I possessed the lonely arrogance of the young drunk
and a pocketful of jukebox change.

On Sunday afternoons, the bar nearly empty,
I drained my pockets.

I don't believe in ranking angels or saints.
Memorizing prayers or counting sins.

/ / /

Our children stand silent as I collapse
the crib. I took my wife's somber picture

as she stood under an umbrella staring
at nothing at a bus stop near the Forum's ruins.

/ / /

One day, the tiles come crashing down.
I said I wasn't me, draining my beer,

slipping down the street to a darker bar
with louder music and cheaper drinks.

/ / /

The kids and I collect sunshine in baskets
beneath our cracked stained-glass window.

During thunderstorms, my son tapes notes
to the glass, asking the rain to stop.

I have witnessed two children emerge screaming
into the world. Sometimes they hug each other

for the hell of it. My wife waits at the bottom
of the stairs to take the screwdriver from my hand.

Soon they will be too old to collect sun.
We'll just have to stand and watch them

in the remaining light.

My son wants to be a detective or spy.
He wants to know what sexual abuse is.
We've purchased two books to teach him
about sex: *It's So Amazing* and
It's Perfectly Normal. I'm not sure
which comes first. What about
It's So Perfectly Amazing? We're
on the way home from a hockey game,
2–2 tie. Free bobbleheads of a star player
recently traded. No predicting shit
like that. Though I don't say *shit*
to him. Sex isn't a bad word, though
a lot of words about sex are bad words
often used when *not* talking
about sex.

      Get it? Do you have to be
in the army to be a spy? No. Just don't
get any tattoos. The tattooed guy behind us
was saying *fuck this* and *fuckin' that*
and I should've said something to him
but he and his buddies outweighed me
by four thousand pounds. Another lesson
there, I explain in traffic. My son was conceived
at a B & B in Key West run by two extremely
nice guys.

      An impatient woman nearly
ran us over, trying to break through the stream
of exiting fans at the crosswalk. A nice
policeman pounded on her hood and had
a word or two with her that may have been
sex words used in a not-sexual context.
When we get home, I'll have to sort out

Perfectly and *Amazing* and lay one on him
to read in the morning. The scoreboard
demanded that we cheer and scream
Loud! and LOUDER! You don't have to do
something just because a grown-up tells you to.
Yes, you can still touch *me*. Just not *there*.
The genitals. Your penis, you know? Some people
take their bobbleheads with them to the bathroom
so no one will steal them. Something wrong
if we can't even leave our bobbleheads in our seats
to take a pee. Solve *that* mystery. No fights
in the game, or in the stands, and that's
a victory for something. We can't find
the post-game show on the car radio,
but if we tilt our heads and look up,
we can half see the half moon above us.

NOCTURNE IN BLUE

On Atwood Street in Pittsburgh
my brother and his two sons from Detroit
walk with me down one side of the street.

Four young black men approach
on the same side of the street.
Late on an empty block.

My brother slants his eyes into mine.
His boys look up at us. We cross
to the other side. Keep on walking.

Perhaps they are relieved. Perhaps
disappointed. We eye them across
the empty street. I have no idea.

The night holds up its empty hands
and the moon bites its lip. Nobody
touches. Our shadows stretch behind us

under the quiet buzz of streetlights.
We breathe, continue to breathe.
The stars sting our skins.

All of us, on Atwood, in Pittsburgh.
In front of us, the sidewalk narrows
until there is room for no one.

You can't sled everywhere in America.
You need a hill. You need snow.

On the way home, two cop cars blocked
our street, their bodies askew, lights

wowing the icy January air. I swerved
around the back way, and bounced

up my driveway, hiding from what-
ever it was. Good old home. Semi-

sweet. Etc. This afternoon two parents
came to blows on the sledding hill,

ignoring the child with the head wound.
I wanted to write *nearly*. My daughter

and I pulled away as the ambulance
arrived. As the police arrived.

My daughter had been pleased
that we'd slid all the way down

into the hay barrels stacked at the bottom
to keep us safe. She'd never seen adults

actually come to blows. Her face was torn
with it, the awkward mashing of flesh

as they aimed at each other's heads,
the vulnerable unpadded place.

You can't sled everywhere in America.
You need—outside, tires are spinning on ice—

you need an alternate route. Climbing back
up the hill, my daughter tired. *That's*

always part of the story, I told her
on the way home, the car heating up

slowly, evening light quickly fading,
nearly immediate night. She talked about

the advantages of sitting in front of the sled
vs. sitting behind me. I didn't want her

to see that: two mad men flailing
against each other, sliding and tumbling

down the hill together while the world
stopped to blow on its cold hands.

A nurse tended to that injured child
while I tended to mine. You need a hill.

You need snow. You need a warm
place to go. *And now this,* my daughter said

as I circled the block. We didn't know what
this was. We'd had enough for one day.

Why do we hit each other? Why couldn't I pull her
up the hill like I did last year? If we had a fireplace,

I would build one. We sat on our old yellow
kitchen floor pulling off boots.

I don't know, I usually ran, I told her,
my face burning. I saw everything

and nothing. You need a way to steer,
or all the room in the world.

Yesterday a guy cut down the big tree
in front of the apartments across the street

and hauled away the wood in his pickup.
March 1. For no good reason. Well, he

got paid, that's his reason. I call the building
owner *they*. The owner's never been identified

on the premises. He had some guy paint
in bright road-yellow NO PARKING directly

on the street. What if everybody did that?
What if Johnny No-Parking traveled the country

painting NO PARKING on every curbside
in front of every house in America? You live

in a city? You know people kill over parking.
Here, we've got the parking chair. You put it

in front of your house and dare anyone to move it.
What's he going to do with all that wood?

The owner just eliminated a nice chunk of shade
for half his tiny box apartments this summer.

They're going to pave over everything. One person
who owns 32 units is a *they*. The tree would have

flowered in about three weeks. Looking at them
every day, you can get attached to other people's

trees. One man with a chainsaw is a *he*
with an asterisk. Depending on how much gas

and his intentions. The crude giant yellow letters
mock me, more visible now than ever. I imagine

it reads NO BARKING just to make me laugh,
just so I don't miss the flowers that were

on their way.

This morning, traffic spaces
itself out with the random logic
of breaking waves.

Last night I asked a young man
to turn down his music,
bass shaking my windows and dishes,
my concentration, my heart.

He was sitting on the steps
near his SUV with a woman
from the apartment building
and her young daughter.

I didn't see them in the shade.
I saw a dark empty vehicle
vibrating the night off its hinges.

He startled me, emerging
from shadow as I approached.
I didn't understand how they could
sit so close nor how such a young man
could afford such an expensive vehicle.

My wife thought it was coming
from an apartment, but I thought a car.
I was checking so when I called the cops
I could tell them what planet I was on.

I've never made noise that loud
though maybe if I had hyper bass
I would've used it on occasion
when the world was a splatter or blur.

This morning among the traffic waves,
no sign of the SUV. Birds in the tree
out front squabbling over something.
So many languages I'll never know.

He turned the music off
without a word. Not down, but off.
What random logic tonight will bring,
I cannot say. I walked back in the house
and turned my porch light on,

a word from a language I learned
as a child. I don't have much funk left
in my system, and my bones benefit
from a random jangle now and then.

Walking back to the house,
I spotted my children at their windows
above me. No one could have slept through
that earth-moving stereo. If sound could dig,
we would've been at the molten core.

The world is a pocket
and most of us are tarnished pennies,
or the world is a book and we are
hyphens in white space. If we turned
sideways, we'd disappear.

The hip-hop words were thick chunks
of sound, vocal bombs, heat-seeking missiles.
We are both against disappearance,
me and the nameless young man
and whatever triangulation exists
between him and the others.

I said please and thank you,
which translates as don't shoot me.
So, I didn't call the police, and the moon
was silent, and the stars were invisible
as they always are in this sad old city.

The day starts, tinny and warm on the boulevard,
cars heading into town in their rush-hour sighs.
Somewhere in the distance,
the signals are changing.

Our neighbors' beans grow through the fence.
Cindy said we could pick the ones on our side.

Last night I heard her yelling through the two
layers of brick that separate our houses—

Go ahead, leave, go out and find wife number four,
you shithead! I laughed aloud next to my sleeping

wife. The kind of laugh—
you shake your head, glad it's not you.

I'd been leaving the beans till they grew
fat, bumpy, inedible. Today I pick them all

and hand them over the fence.
You guys need them more, I say. Steve's sledge-

hammering something in their bathroom.
Our hot street holds no secrets. Open windows

feed the mirage of a breeze. This morning,
dried sweat salted lines on our black sheets.

My wife threatens to call the police, or worse,
tell them directly to stop the screaming.

They're scaring our children. *We just yell a lot,*
Cindy tells me, as if that explains everything.

You guys are so quiet over there
we think you must be dead sometimes.

I think we're alive. I sing my children to sleep
with the Canadian national anthem.

Maybe we're just Canadian inside. I hope so.
Canada has a small army and no magic bombs.

Cindy and Steve joined the Syrian Orthodox Church
around the corner, though they're neither Syrian

nor Orthodox. For years, I've been trying to get rid
of the morning glories in our yard. It's impossible.

And now, my daughter, four, gleefully points out
each new blossom. I will stop pulling them up.

They're trying, next door. We're trying here.
Nothing's Orthodox in this city of tilted chimneys,

soot-stained bricks. Weeks later, I'll spot Cindy
reaching pudgy fingers through the fence

to get those beans on our side. Today, she takes
them from my outstretched hands.

I can barely breathe, she says.
Maybe it'll cool off tonight, I say.

We both look up at the hazy sun. A bus rumbles
up the hill behind us. It is never quiet here.

Climbing to retrieve my son's ball
in a neighbor's yard, I caught
my wedding ring on the fence

and nearly ripped my finger off.
Fifteen years ago, my wife's name
engraved inside by a jeweler friend

of her cousin in Zagreb. I desperately
tried to unhook myself before I passed out.
The jeweler knew how to spell Kovacic

but hadn't a clue about Daniels. We got a laugh
out of that. Her cousin Neven died in the war
during the siege of Vukovar.

He was married and had a young son
who now stutters and lives in a land
of bad cartoons. His widow's trapped

in her mother-in-law's apartment. Last year
we returned to the tiny rooms
of Neven's life,

stepping over decapitated
dolls and angry scribbles.
                          My wedding
ring was salvaged, a slight bend where

it snagged.
                 Though we were not yet
married, we wore the rings in Zagreb.
The family gave us small presents to wedge

into our luggage. I bent the hands
of the clock, and it never worked.
I forgot about retrieving the ball.

I sometimes forget about Neven.
We sent wads of cash during the war—
in multiple envelopes, hoping some

would get through. We'd bought the rings
after changing too many dollars
into dinars. We couldn't change them

back. In the city then, Yugoslavia was
one endless cheap cigarette. In the country,
one long black dusty skirt. Tito

was a feared god, and TV made up Partisan
bios for the high politicos. Fairy tales
from American rock bands were imported

as sacred tracts. Us, we were buying gold.
Circles with our names inscribed so we
would not forget. Her history numbed me.

We held hands like scared teenagers.
Forgetting was either an art form
or the biggest sin. Neven wouldn't join

the Party. He loved his dog Whisky
with the wadded currency of his heart.
The government snipped zeroes off the money

like a blind barber, so you never knew what
you had. Tito'd made his grandfather disappear.
The country was full of black magic

and we were buying gold with soiled bills
under a slanted sun and the ever-
present portrait of Tito.

My finger
does not bend all the way, though the ring
fits over the scar. I only hung from the fence

a few brief seconds, though Neven
would have said
it was all the time in the world.

My children and I color the flags
of imagined countries. We watch

sleeping tenants across the street
through sliding glass doors. Few bother

with curtains. Few have anywhere to go
for work. My son said *cocaine*

for the first time today, singing
"I Get a Kick Out of You"

from *Anything Goes*. Last week
we walked downtown to see it.

He's almost seven. She's five. The names
of our new countries are unimportantly

clever, our little secrets. *Wake up, sleepyheads,*
we sing softly. They're not far away,

the lives across the street. We're up early
here. Our flags are sprinkled with kisses,

eggs, eyeglasses, water, grass. My son
has 3-D glasses. My daughter, a whoopee

cushion. The instructions on my new socks
say *Do Not Eat*. We use invisible glue and tape.

An exterminator shows up across the street.
My flag is a big bar of soap. The country

of Happiness Soap—I could never keep
a secret. I do not know their names

across the street. Last week someone lost
his life over there. No flagpole within blocks

of here, but perhaps a thousand invisible borders.
Excuse me for being imprecise. My daughter colors

a flag of hearts, but we cannot give a name
to our own country.

ACKNOWLEDGMENTS

Antioch Review: "Vitamins"

Blue Collar Review: "Bridal Dance"

Cimarron Review: "Sizing the Ring"

Comstock Review: "Esperanza"

Confrontation: "Illuminating the Saints"

Crazyhorse: "Mystery Seeds"

The Florida Review: "Imperfectly"

Flyway: "Todi Landscape"

The Georgia Review: "American Dream"

Green Mountains Review: "Cry Room, St. Mark's Church," "Wonder"

Gulf Coast: The Land of 3000 Dreams"

Hunger Mountain: "The ability of the corpse"

The Indiana Review: "You bring out the boring white guy in me,"
   "These days they're wearing their haloes tight"

King Log: "Mending Fences"

Labor: "Rocking at the DQ"

Natural Bridge: "Ringing Doorbells"

North American Review: "Poetry"

Northwest Review: "Flags"

The Paterson Literary Review: "Dim," "Outdoor Chef"

Pearl: "Capital Punishment: Lethal Injection"

Pemmican: "Revolt of the Crash-Test Dummies," "Nocturne in Blue"

Phi Kappa Phi Forum: "Big Bang"

Pleiades : "Charles Holmes blew up the chem lab"

Ploughshares: "Engraving"

Poet Lore: "¿"

Poetry International : "Take Your Pills"

Poetry Miscellany: "Hung Out to Dry"

The Rio Grande Review: "Summer Strike at the Axle Plant"

River Styx: "Efficiency, Bowling Green, OH"

The Seattle Review: "White Crayon"

Seneca Review: "Sledding in America"

Slipstream: "Explicit"

Smartish Pace: "Waiting Room, Children's Hospital, Pittsburgh"

Water-Stone: "They"

Yale Review: "Firing the Late Person"

A native of Detroit, Jim Daniels now lives in Pittsburgh.
He is the Thomas Stockham Baker Professor of English at
Carnegie Mellon University, where he teaches in the
creative writing program. The recipient of numerous
awards, including the Brittingham Prize for Poetry,
Jim Daniels has published three volumes of short fiction
and nine collections of poems, among them *Show and
Tell: New and Selected Poems* (2003), which was a finalist
for the Paterson Poetry Prize. He has also written the
screenplays for two independent feature films, *No Pets*
(1994) and *Dumpster* (2005), and is the author of a
one-act play, *Heart of Hearts*, which was produced at
New York's 13th Street Repertory Theater in 1998. His
poems have appeared widely and have been featured in
the *Pushcart Prize* and *Best American Poetry* anthologies.